better together*

*This book is best read together, grownup and kid.

 akidsco.com

a kids book about

a kids book about CONSTRUCTION

by Andrew Colas
in partnership with Colas Construction

a kids book about

Printed in the United States of America.

A Kids Book About books are available online: *akidsco.com*

To share your stories, ask questions, or inquire about bulk
purchases (schools, libraries, and nonprofits), please use
the following email address: *hello@akidsco.com*

Print ISBN: 978-1-958825-81-5
Ebook ISBN: 978-1-958825-82-2

Designed by Jelani Memory
Edited by Emma Wolf

The author would like to thank fellow authors, Aneshka Colas-Dickson,
Alexander Colas, Marc-Daniel Domond, and Haleah Blank. Each shared
in the collaborative process of this book, a special endeavor to honor
the founders of Colas Construction and the construction industry.

To my father, Hermann Colas, Jr., the founder of Colas Construction, whose vision to uplift the community grew into a successful family-owned and operated commercial construction firm.

To my mother, Roberta Colas, who helped forge the foundation of COLAS with her beloved husband, Hermann.

Together, they established strong roots that grew with passion, courage, and perseverance.

Intro

For the kid in your life: Do you like to draw shapes and create fresh ideas? Jump into the exciting world of building with Colas Construction and let your imagination inspire your next construction project!

The COLAS team is driven to build construction projects that uplift and serve our community. From building homes, to schools, to landmarks like the Oregon Convention Center, we're committed to building spaces that leave a lasting impact.

Embark on this educational adventure with *A Kids Book About Construction*—a book that not only strives to entertain but nurture curiosity and instill the drive to explore. As you read, you'll learn a ton about construction, where ideas turn into reality with dedication and teamwork.

Let the construction adventures begin!

Hey, kid! Yes, **YOU**!

This book is all about **construction**.

Most grownups think construction is loud, messy, expensive, and takes a loooooooong time.

To be honest, **they're not wrong**.

What kids understand that grownups often don't...is construction is **actually incredible**!

But let's not get ahead of ourselves. Let's start with what construction is.

Look around the room you're in.

What do you see?
Lights? Walls? Is it warm? Cold?
There's probably a floor, right?!

ALL OF THIS IS PART

OF CONSTRUCTION.

But construction is also so much more!

CONSTRUCTION SHAPES ALMOST THE ENTIRE WORLD AROUND YOU AND HAS EXISTED FOREVER!

Because of construction...

Your favorite athlete has a **stadium** to play their sport.

You have a **school** to go to.

Your favorite musician or band has a **stage** to perform on.

You have a **home** to live in.

That's right,

CONSTRUCTION IS EVERYWHERE!

And every **construction project** starts with a need.

For example, maybe your neighborhood needs a new school.

First, an **architect** creates a design for what the school will look like and how it will work.

Then, an **engineer** makes sure the design for the school will keep people safe.

Next, the **contractor** makes the plan for how the school will get built and finds the team to do it.

Together, they work to decide the materials to use, when construction will happen, and how much it will cost.

They ask important questions like:

What makes a good school?

How big should the gym be?

How many kids should
fit in the cafeteria?

Where will accessibility
ramps be placed?

...and about 100 more
questions just like those!

Everyone works together to create a space where kids can learn, play, and grow!

Now that they have their **plan**,
it's time to **build**!

Building begins with **earthwork**.

Excavation operators use big machines that scoop, lift, and dig to reshape the land.

Utilities like electrical, sewer, water, and the internet (really important stuff!) go in the ground.

Then, it's time to form and pour the **concrete foundation**.

The **foundation** is what the whole building sits on.

Even though **so much work** has already been done, at this point, it may look like nothing has really changed.

But this is what's amazing
about construction:

THERE ARE SO MANY PIECES, BIG AND SMALL, AND EACH ONE IS VERY IMPORTANT.

With a solid foundation,
now comes the fun part!

The structure goes up and the building takes shape with its walls and windows.

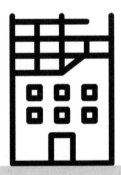

Once the structure is built, the roof goes on and the construction team has a celebration called the "Top Out."

It's important to acknowledge milestones during loooooong projects!

Next comes something
called the "rough-in."

This is when all the hidden materials get installed behind the walls, like wires, pipes, insulation, and ducts.*

*not quacking ducks!

At last come the "finishes."
This includes those final
touches that make everything
look just right, as planned.

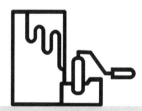

SHINY AND BRIGHT! IT EVEN SMELLS BRAND-NEW.

Lights go in, as well as doors, windows, grass, a playground, basketball hoops—you name it!

THAT'S A LOT, RIGHT?!

It takes the hands of many people to do all that work.

And each person who works in construction is incredibly important, and part of the team.

Many get to work on-site during construction, and there are more working behind the scenes at the office.

The **Project Manager, Superintendent**, and **Project Engineer** are a few of the leaders who are responsible for building the project on the construction site.

Then there are all the **tradespeople** who do work on specific parts of the building like **plumbers, electricians, carpenters, roofers, painters,** and **so many more.**

And every day, for 1, 2, or more years, hundreds of people show up to make this new structure a reality.

ISN'T THAT REMARKABLE?

And they all bring different skills, ideas, and expertise to make it happen.

CONSTRUCTION CAN BE BUSY.

CONSTRUCTION CAN BE LOUD.

Construction can look different

EVERY DAY.

But one thing is for certain: construction is never boring!

This might seem like a lot of work and time just to make 1 building.

But guess what!?

IT WILL LAST A LIFETIME!

And that's the

MAGIC OF CONSTRUCTION!

Construction builds places and spaces we use every day.

Like our homes, parks, hospitals, stadiums, and more to meet our needs and help build community, which makes our lives better.

As what we need changes,
so does construction.

That's why we see new buildings, bridges, and roads being built

ALL THE TIME.

So next time, if your grownup gets annoyed in a construction zone, remind them of the magic by saying...

"YOU'RE LOOKING AT AN IDEA COMING TO LIFE!"

Outro

Did you know that you're a natural builder? Whether stacking blocks or tinkering with ideas, construction can make a pillow fort, cardboard spaceship, lemonade stand, and more—let your imagination run wild! Maybe one day, you'll even build a home for a family!

Ready for more construction adventures? Explore these exciting questions:

What tools do construction workers use?

How do construction vehicles work, like cranes and bulldozers?

Can kids become construction workers when they grow up?

The world of construction is fun, inspiring, and rewarding. This diverse industry builds amazing projects. And guess what? Anyone can be a part of it. Embrace the excitement of construction and help build a brighter future, today. Let's make your construction dreams come true!

About The Author

Meet Andrew Colas and Colas Construction, your friendly construction experts! Growing up, watching construction projects come to life with his dad inspired Andrew's future as a leader at COLAS with his siblings and cousin. Andrew recalls his father always talking about vision, belief, and determination. He said no matter what you see and what isn't there, you can change the future—you can change the system.

Within the pages of this book, discover the world of construction and how rewarding our industry is. We're proud to be part of it! We can create homes, schools, and an entire neighborhood! The COLAS team is proud to have a lasting impact in the Pacific Northwest and globally and to inspire the next generation to dive into the world of construction.

 @colasconstruction   @colasconstruction

 colasconstruction.com

kids
book
about
ONEY

by Stromwasser

kids
book
about
BEING
INCLUSIVE

by Ashton Mota
& Rebekah Bruesehoff

kids
book
about
diversity

kids
book
about
LEADER
SHIP

by Orion Jean

kids
boo
abo
IMMI

by MJ Calder

a
kids
book
about
CLIMATE
CHANGE

by Zanagee Artis
Olivia Greenspan

a
kids
book
about
IMAGINATION

by LEVAR BURTON

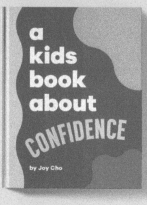
a
kids
book
about
CONFIDENCE

by Joy Cho

a
ki
ba
S

by E

ds
ok
out
XIETY

zabo
d Happy Faces

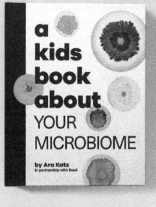
a
kids
book
about
YOUR
MICROBIOME

by Ara Katz
In partnership with Seed

a
kids
book
about
racism

by Jelani Memory

a
kids
book
about
DISABILITIES

by Kristine Napper

a
kid
boo
abo
bore

by: KYLE ST

a
kids
book
about
IVORCE

by Ashley Simpo

a
kids
book
about
cancer

by Dr. Kelsie Storm & Sarah Porter

a
kids
book
about
BEING
TRANSGENDER

by Gia Parr
in partnership with The GenderCool Project

a
kids
book
about
DEPRESSION

by Kileah McIlvain

a
ki
be
al

by Mel

ds
ok
ut
ame

a
kids
book
about
THE TULSA
RACE MASSACRE

**Discover more
at akidsco.com**